ANTHOLOGY OF POEMS FOR GREENSPIRITS

*To Grace,
with love from
Joan.
Thank you for your poems.*

GreenSpirit book series

Anthology *of* Poems for GreenSpirits

Compiled by Joan Angus

Independent Publishing Platform
Distributed and printed by Amazon

Title No. 11 in the GreenSpirit Book Series
www.greenspirit.org.uk
GreenSpirit is a registered charity based in the UK. The main contents/written
material, editing, design and promotional work for its books is done on a purely
voluntary basis or given freely by contributors who share a passion for
Gaia-centred spirituality.

© anthology, Joan Angus 2020
Individual copyright belongs to the majority of authors used in this anthology.

First edition
ISBN 9798676939113
A low-cost eBook edition of *Anthology of Poems for GreenSpirits* is also available.

All rights reserved. Except for brief quotations in critical articles or reviews,
no part of this book may be reproduced in any manner without prior written
permission from the compiler.

Design and artwork by Santoshan (Stephen Wollaston)

Cover and title page illustration © November_Seventeen/Shutterstock.com

Page 55 and 56 photo © Sergey Nivens/Shutterstock.com
Page 149 and 150 image © Mopic/Shutterstock.com

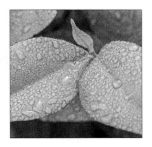

Contents

Introduction 7
1. Life's Journeys 9
2. Musing, Meditation and Isness 25
3. Visits to Places 37
4. Lifestyle 55
5. Relationships 75
6. Seasons 89
7. Meetings with Natures' Community 115
8. Healing 137
9. Humanity's Environmental Cruelty and Destruction 149
Conclusion 163
Biographies 167
GreenSpirit Resources 183

Introduction

Welcome to my gathering of poems for GreenSpirits. Most of them have already been published in our magazines over the years. Some have been contributed by friends of GreenSpirits and most by members.

I have enjoyed reading the poems and regret having to reject some for a variety of reasons. Thank you to all the contributors. Your poems are truly inspiring. Keep writing and if any others of you are inspired by this book please let me know. I will continue to collect poems for the GreenSpirit magazine.

~ Joan Angus

Life's Journeys

1

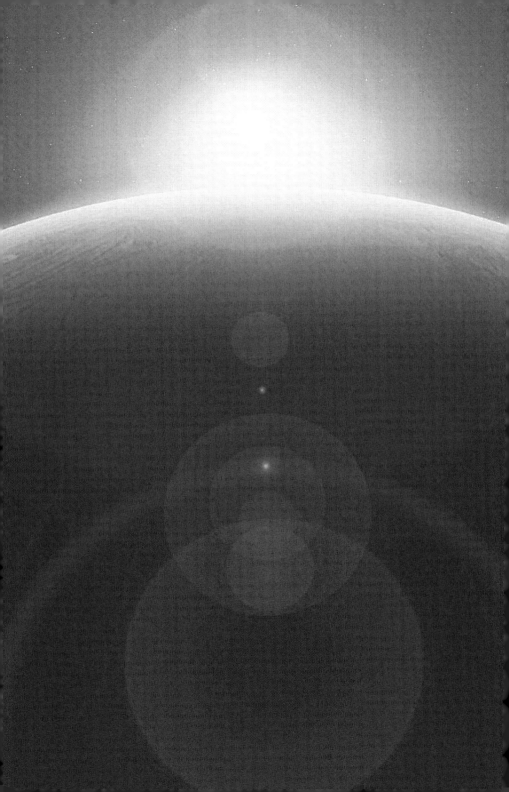

Ode to Creation Spirituality

The Earth is our Mother
We are her kin
Our Father who loves us
Dwells there within
Thru Creation and Science they say we are one
with the trees, the stars and even the sun
They say life's a blessing
not about sin
That the child inside us
needs to come out and win
If we take heed of their wisdom
we'll be changed and be healed
And that is where our gifts are revealed
For when we're reborn in the truth of it all
we know its about compassion not the fall
And when we can trust what we have been told
we give birth to a power that's more precious than gold.

~ Margie Schneider

Big Bang Poem

Once before time was
there existed a full stop
and within this tiny .
sat all that was,
is and shall be

So weighted and full was it
that finally
    it burst
and out fell everything
with an almighty surge

And all that was, is and
Shall be, was sent spinning:

Children's tops
a tropical night
    full of Jaguar's eyes
musical notation
you and me
grasshoppers, oak trees
the Milky Way
head lice, the Grand Canyon
kingfishers, brimstone butterflies
lapis lazuli, cox's pippins
Stonehenge, pasque flowers
Maria Callas.

~ Richard Meyers

I shall lay down my compass

I shall stop reading my compass,
Twisting it this way and that,
Watching the metallic blue needle
Make the decisions. Instead,
I shall lay a finger on my pulse,
Sniff the wind, pick flowers,
Feel the balance and recoil of affinities –
Consult oracles.

Very deep the seed with a voice
Like the sound of a waterfall
Cries to be born.
The clear light trapped in the stone
With long low cadences
Vibrates the silver cord in my hand.

I shall lay down my compass,
I shall follow a new path.
Who said I needed to go North?

~ Grace Blindell

Path to the Beach

Only one path
led to that beach, and that one hidden well
in folds of thicket, past a waterhole, through trees
arching, dark like dusk. Only the salty smell
and growing sandiness beneath your feet
disclosed the secret, if you thought to look. But then,
around the turn, and suddenly a roar –
and the whole sky broke open to reveal
infinity of blue and gold and blue.
What to do? What can you do, on such a strand except
run, dance with the wind, fling off your clothes, whirl naked, sing?
Flirt with the whispering foam, and laughing, stand
as the tide steals sand from under your very soles.
Seek treasure here, tossed wide by a spendthrift sea.
Or lie with your lover in those sculpted dunes.
Make love to him, or her, the sun, or both, or none.

LIFE'S JOURNEYS

And maybe weep because when all is done
you have to choose a path. There will be one
too dangerous to take. It is the siren way, with charms that
    bid you run
and dance one perfect, final pirouette into the ocean's arms
in ultimate surrender. Any action less complete than that,
    is compromise. But you will take the long way home,
follow your own, oncoming footprints in damp sand,
clutching your shell, your prize of cuttlefish,
your bittersweet, unconsummated dream.
Only one path
led to that beach. And that one hidden now
in folds of history. You cannot go again.
Someone has bought the land, and now the sand
is strewn with deck chairs. Now the whirling, sighing wind
that whisked your hair, and chimed the siren's bell
(now a mere echo in your long-dried shell),
plays for the dance no more.
The chance is gone.

~ Marian Van Eyk McCain

Edge

That scary place, the edge, is where it happens,
Like dance arising from stillness,
Or sound from silence.
The edge, where nothing is, is where everything begins.

If you want to avoid being at the edge
Then you must hold the earthquake at bay,
Stifle the volcano. Yes, you single-handed
Must deny that important emergence.
You think you can do that? The tectonic plates can't
And they are vaster, older, and more experienced than you.

The tectonic plates, riding the pulse of the molten core
Bump and buffet together, raw edges,
Hidden, terrifying, deep, mysterious,
They are nevertheless where newness comes.

The molten possibility dreams itself into being at the margins,
The red hot stream of 'what might be' mounts upward.
But only through the torn and wounded edge
flows into new being
that pool of potentiality, which will be the future,
is born at the extremity.

Both burdened and endowed with choice, the human
Stands – poised always at the brink.
The stream of possibility flows on
Unending. It throbs and calls in every living cell
Seeking its own potential, whilst the edge –
Always and everywhere – offers risk.

~ Grace Blindell

*   *   *

The Oaks on the Common

The oaks on the common are dancing,
With every week they shift their weight upon the ground.
With every month they swirl their garments,
and in the year reach out to their friends.
There is but one majestic step throughout their age,
in which they open out the centuries to their death.

~ Chris Clarke

Morning Mist

Dark.
A glow on the horizon.
The mountain shrugs a billow of mist
    from his shoulders,
raises his tousled heathery head
to greet a new day.
His downy cover rolls back
sinking into the valley below.

A pinkness blushes the sky
greeted by the birds' Matins song.
All life below is smothered
By the rolling blanket;
a pearly world of dimly seen shapes,
damp branches,
dripping twigs.

The dew drenched road disappears
in the greyed air.
Follow that road.
Do not stray into the grey.
Strive on up, feeling the way
to encounter revelation,
a new vision, clarity of sight.

~ Sarah Jane Toleman

These Days

Summer mellows into autumn
Conkers and beech mast underfoot,
Shiny plump blackberries there for the taking
And birds sing to celebrate the harvest.

My pace is slower these days
I pause to absorb the magic,
Ponder on summer's spent promises
And celebrate the abundance of my life.

Where did the summer go?
I can still dance when the music plays.
But perhaps if I take my time
There will be longer to savour the autumn.

~ Joan Angus

Final Moments

In blind return to the Atlantic womb,
This eager stream has furrowed to the shore,
Through green, sheep-sprinkled, Devon hills, a combe
Lush lined with oak and beech and sycamore.

Deep in this fold, her journey's legacy
Of silt to ferns bequeathed, her life's tales told,
She flows with softness, equanimity.
Her waters light; no burden left to hold.

Suddenly, now! She rounds the combe's last bend
A dozen yards from where the breakers crash.
The last tree passed. Salt stings the air. The end.
Time now to make that final, trembling dash

Through hard, grey rock, where gulls scream at the sun,
Die to herself, and open to the One.

~ Marian Van Eyk McCain

Nunc Dimittis

There are many departures in this life,
times when we have to let go
of something or someone
perhaps treasured beyond measure;
partings that are, if we knew it, a preparation
for that final farewell
When all joys and sorrows of worldly being cease and
God willing, we can depart in peace
according to thy word…
And there have been those moments
when I have seen or felt,
in the cycle of the seasons,
the certainty of day passing into night,
in the inevitable movement of the stars,
in the irresistible migration of birds,
in the sure bright flourishing & decay of the sun flower,
a kind of glorious inexorable rhythm to life
that hints at salvation,
That offers glimpses of a higher reality,
a unity just beyond imagination's reach

~ Peter Watkins

Sarajevo Marketplace – A mother

In line the unthinkable
Thought considered and accepted
(she will queue for food)
As the shell explodes.
In the silence
Before the screams, before
The prurience of press and newsreel
Who can tell what her thoughts are?
Quiet moments of delight
And play in the corn
Skylark directly overhead
Full of song.

~ Richard Meyers

The Death of a Bee

Yesterday I picked up a Bee.
No…I picked up the discarded packaging
Of a Bee.
That lovely buzzing honey-bewitched dynamo
Had left.
That which inspired all the summer-long busy-ness,
Vitalised every hair of its stripey furriness,
Tuned its sensitive direction-finding antennae,
Given it purpose,
Had gone.
Cast off was this dry, lightweight,
Folded up carcass.
Delicate, fascinating in its complexity,
But quite lifeless.

How was its leaving?
The separation of Bee-spirit, Bee-person,
From Bee-body?
Did it know its desolation at the end?
Or was there acceptance of change?

How is all our leaving?
Do we weep for our known faithful body's passing?
Fearing the return of substance to its origin,
Confusing that which has grown old and needs to pass
With that which has never grown old…
Nor ever will.

~ Grace Blindell

Beltane Burial, 3rd May 2019
In memory of Chris Clarke

We follow him in his coffin,
covered in a blanket of lilac,
pulled on a cart down the steep hill
to his place of burial in the shimmering woodland.

We gather round the grave.
He is lowered gently into his resting place
'Earth to earth…dust to dust…'
Pipe music plays a lullaby.

Raindrops fall through the canopy of young green leaves
'Earth my body, Water my blood,
Air my breath and Fire my spirit'
We throw handfuls of soil in farewell
and leave to the beat of a drum.

What will your spirit do, dear Friend, when we have left?
Will you dance with other spirits
in the woodland
for ever?

~ Joan Angus

Musings, Meditations and Isness

2

MUSING, MEDITATION AND ISNESS

If our sight could not reach to the Sun,
Our knowing could never embrace it:
And if God's work moved not in us,
Then how could we delight in it?

~ After Goethe, *translation by Chris Clarke*

*　　*　　*

What I Think about When I Run

I like it best when I am headless so to speak,
My body just runs
In an economy of effort,
Knowing perfectly well how to keep in balance
My heart, my lungs and my muscles,
Leaving my conscious mind free to drift.

I like it best when it drifts off nowhere so to speak,
Into empty space,
Then sometimes what has been missing is found,
What is stuck becomes unstuck,
The insurmountable become surmountable;
A kind of unravelling of knots
As I run

So to speak.

~ Peter Watkins

Sometimes I Think

Sometimes I think
That the daisies during the day
Are mirroring the stars at night.
Or maybe they are the stars
Reflecting themselves.
I almost trod on the Pleiades yesterday
As I walked over the green and white spangled surface
Of our world.

The daisies – so dear and yet so ordinary
Flung broadcast over the earth
As the stars across the sky,
Yet each its own self.
Interdependent, co-arising,
The daisies, the stars you, me,
This tree, that comet.

~ Grace Blindell

MUSING, MEDITATION AND ISNESS

Can we know God?

Do we need to fully know a dragonfly
to glory in its iridescent wings?
Or a sunbeam
to feel comfort in its rays?
Do we need to fully know our friends
to feel love for them?

We, who cannot even fully know ourselves;
we do not have an understanding
of the length of years,
the endless wonder of our planet
or to grasp the span of universe.

But we can know God
in the colours of the rainbow,
the running of the deer,
the grandeur of the mountains
and the touch and smile of friends.

~ Sarah Jane Toleman

Walking at Sunset in Winter

The world at three miles an hour
offers itself in such richness
I almost can't take it in.
The retreating tide has left its fingerprints
in the estuary sand –
The geese have returned from Siberia
and murmur in great flocks on the fields –
The sun glows low in the west –
The sky is a powder blue –
The cumuli rose tinted –
Trees are filigreed in the fading light –
Out on the mudflats a curlew cries hauntingly.

In the immensity of this moment
I could happily lay down my life.

~ Peter Watkins

Today

Today had ended fraught, and so
I took my accustomed tree-lined walk.
This was enough.
And all the trees were bare to me:
This was enough.
Then walking on the single track
back home, I entered there.
That was enough.

~ Chris Clarke

Before the Storm

Exulting steel powerclouds over the wood
Light strained through transforms colour
Behind the farmhouse Scots pines are black skeletons
Shouting orange rooftiles are glowing rose
In the silence before the storm
Only the cuckoos dare make fun of the world
And skylarks carol in ecstacy
Because they can't bear to stop.
Lightning, a spear thrust lightens my heart –
here it comes!
Look down. The buttercups all move –
Furl themselves shut all together.
The thunder growls and rolls like a rough-haired dog.
Roll in the wet grass with me
Take off those dull heavy clothes
and let clean water beat joyfully on your skin
Kiss me and laugh in the rain.

~ Heather Shute

Singing in December 2012

A bird flies out of the darkness towards the dawn.
The one long note of now
becomes deep sweet song
and all our yesterdays
dance into the distance.

We are standing on the edge of time,
On the edge of a bay lined with
snow-covered mountains.

We are opening up, we are opening up.
This endless journey, made
and made anew. A deeper rhythm. My heartbeat,
water washing on far shores,
the beat of the bird's wings.

Every one of my cells is alight,
Glowing in the shift from soft to
fierce sound. The discovery
of harmony; the found places
to land and be, to sound out, to dance
in the blending of our voices, in the
song of our making.

Around us the world is happening anew. Across the bay
the bird calls out
for her tribe to join her.

~ Bryony Rogers

The Tide Line

Sometimes when I walk to the tide line
Self preoccupation seems to slip away.

Flint pebbles glint in remembrance
of the retreating tide –
corrugated waves ripple towards the shore
with a long sigh –
the firm smooth sand is
studded with cockle shells –
bladderwrack waits at the highest reaches –
oystercatchers fuss and stir.

To fully enter this moment
is a kind of bliss.

A distant clock tower chimes and
I look back at the empty footprints in the sand.

~ Peter Watkins

Watching Clouds

Through a hole in huge dark clouds,
tiny puffy ones shine.
Beyond, in the daylight,
solid blue obscures millions of invisible stars.
That unyielding dome is nothing.
I'm being entertained by an unbelievable movie.
Fast, and low, the white wisps move,
hiding then exposing glimpses of heaven's expanse.
Now, dark clouds seem like impenetrable walls.
The joy of shifting floating layers are contrasted
by multi-backdrops of differing shapes,
Smokey or silver-rimmed.
Moments like these will last for ever.

~ Ruth Barton

Mist! Gently keeping quietness
around the trees and houses,
drawing the scope of the seen world
into a gentle spread of here,
now.

Beyond the visible trees
I knew those unseen
and beyond, those of the town,
planet and so on…

to the all encompassing
ultimate being,
in the beauty of silence.

~ Chris Clarke, from his *Book of Blogs*

Visits to Places

3

Return

As I stand here, I still can see those green
grass hillsides where now mushroom villas crowd;
in my mind's eye and ear, a skylark seen
and heard. Sweet bird, mere dot against a cloud.

But now, by privet hedge, hydrangeas bloom.
"Video library", "Petrol". "For Sale",
the signs scream out. There is no longer room
For the remembered spinney, or its nightingale.

Yet the old beech still stands, and in her bark,
carved long ago by thoughtless, teenaged hand,
my name, scar-tissued to the faintest mark,
may just be traced. At last I understand...

forgiveness. Fifty uncomplaining years
the tree has waited for these healing tears.

~ Marian Van Eyk McCain

Centuries of Men

An old Abbey on a cold winter's night, snow
falling. Centuries of men

wrapped in rough brown cloth
are singing. I wipe tears

from eyes in a white face, ancient, my own. Voices
eco out through the garden, across icy fields,
to the river. Trees
shiver their last leaves, birds hold their breath.

I've been coming here for years, seen the river
cut rock into sand
and run it out to the sea. The men keep singing
Domine Domine. Amongst the trees

by the river, a deer stops. His black eye
holds light

He stands and listens, hears
seeds turn in the black earth, water

running by, and, over us all,
the wide arc of the sky,
the endless stars.

~ Bryony Rogers

Holiday on the Norfolk Coast

The terns turn in the wind
and the pebbles roll,
the sea's heart beating with mine.
The martins scream down wires
into high sandy burrows,
arrows with accurate purpose.

O I love
the brazen gulls,
the huge horizon,
the mystery of moon and tides and
small things hidden in intricate shells.

~ Heather Shute

The Russian Monastery

Hidden among the arid Hebron hills,
Creeping stalagmites of wax contoured the flagstone floors,
Forgotten centuries hung in the dark and rancid air.
With their matted hair and beards,
Their grime encrusted robes, did they know?
Those two remaining monks, living out their shuffling days,
Did they know, the world still turned?
That beauty still burst forth in unexpected places.

In the vastness that is Mother Russia
Are there families still, who have some distant memory
Of brother, uncle, cousin,
Long lost, cut off by ocean, land or revolution?

The place had been sucked down
Into the whirlpool of oblivion,
Drowned aeons ago in the waters of Lethe,
And now, in a mad and twisted time-warp
Doomed forever to live out a slow-motion somnambulism,
An hypnotic re-enactment of empty ritual.

VISITS TO PLACES

Then from this never-never land at noon,
rang out
A single bell. The dark brown tone sprang
Like a shining new-born chestnut from the
tower.
The whole sky trembled – sound waves –
shocked from sleep
Quickened, bunched, then swung
In widening spirals, out and out and out.

Nothing remained unmoved.
The dry and dusty valleys, olive trees,
The stones, and even, hidden by high walls,
The hearts of humans.
I stood, shaken, softened and amazed.

~ Grace Blindell

Watching Nothing Happen

Nothing is ordinary for any length of time.
Behind closed curtains we emerge from sleep.
What have we missed, closed our eyes to?
I stand and see things from another perspective.
Wind and sea throw a thousand glinting diamonds into
    the seaweed.
A wide rainbow sweeps from heaven to earth.
We cast an eye over the rocks.
White froth and grey blue merging.
The shore becomes sea that blends into distant beaches.
Mountains reach to penetrate the sky.
The clouds form a figure seven.
Projected top stroke, lintel-like across a blue entrance into
    the lower heavens.
Sail Mhor's domed summit comes and goes through
    seven's opening.
The people beyond enjoy their pale gold sunrise.
Between two dark cloud strips, blinding rays force their
    way through.
Then we draw back to see the picture from our standpoint.
The great orb thrusts its blinding light upon a stipple-dotted sea.
Waves on the foreshore lap over pebbles.
Heaven's seven dissolves and the clouds regroup.

VISITS TO PLACES

Mist covers the khaki hills of Gruinard Island.
Palpable calm, now the heaviness subsides.
A dusting of snow covers distant peaks.
Three Great Northern Divers, now two, now five.
Heads down, wings back, heads up, look behind, repeat.
As if observing an ancient ritual.
If an otter's head pops up more than once in the same place,
    it's a rock.
If a piece of driftwood floats around in the sea, don't trust it.
It could be an otter in disguise.
When you're gone, he twists and dives deep.
Or drifts with glistening prey clutched in dextrous paws.
He flips round, dives and leaps till he's giddy.
I thought those clouds were mountains.
Like the driftwood that was an otter?
But skyscapes are transitory, and these remain.
The frenetic sky has melded into a light blanket.
Back here the rain's falling oh so gently.
A steady procession of murky foam-topped waves rolls towards us.
What remains of today?
Nothing.
Except a crescent in a diamond encrusted sky.

~ Ruth Barton

Orkney

Wind blows drifts of clouds
revealing a softened,
sheep-clipped green.

A single standing megalith fenced
as though it might walk away
beyond its bounds,
stride across the fields

to a distant ring of stones;
a gathering of giants
reaching into the sky.

~ Sarah Jane Toleman

Henrhyd Waterfall

There is a sense
of spiritual presence
as we enter the wood.
All is still.
The sun pierces the lacy canopy,
leaving patterns
on the trail
down into the ravine.
Suddenly we see her
surrounded
by a rocky amphitheatre;
a princess
lets down her silver tresses
into the black pool below.
Up on the ridge,
a bevy of young oak trees
jostle each other
for the best view.
The sound
of rushing water
echoes round the woodland,
drowning out all other sound.
Leaves on the turn
float down to the river
as she bubbles
over pebbles and rocks
on her way downstream.

~ Joan Angus

The Norbury Erratics

These are huge granite boulders moved by glaciers during
the Ice-age and deposited elsewhere.

Willy-Nilly they came
Each in its own right
An invincible block-buster
Quite unaware of their
Entombment in ice.

Boasting their intractable determination
And steadfast stance
They moved nevertheless
In an ice
Whose cold and immense intention
Outwitted
Their granite perceptions,
As a tidal wave outmanoeuvres
A grain of sand.

Now, on an alien hill
They perch
Preposterous still,
Grinding their granite teeth
In their heavy importance.
Quite blind to the fact
that their whole world
Has melted away.

~ Grace Blindell

VISITS TO PLACES

From *I Colum Cille*: St Columba's Isle
IV: Why We Stayed

It's the glass-blue day
It's the way light inhabits
the creases, smears colour
that steals your breath.

It's the unbidden moment
that spells dolphin, otter, seal.

It's the islands we come to
the islands we're not.

It's the white glyphs
that scribble the swell
In the Sound, and the bucking boats
that yield, and do not sink.

It's the sand so pale
it might be grains of light.

It's the big Hebridean night
that opens its arms
and drops its creels of stars
towards our upturned faces.

~ Roselle Angwin

Wayland's Smithy Revisited

I returned, remembering an earlier
time. When there was a magic
So sharp and clear, so tangible,
It caught my breath and beat my pulse
To its own different rhythm.

But this time not coming
In expectation of gifts,
These had already been given. Instead
I returned to honour
A place that was somehow spirit-filled
Whether I felt it so, or no.

And so I trod the pounded chalk.
Butterflies, their wings spread wide along the way
Jewelled the whitened track.
A solitary bird called and clattered in the hedge,
I reached the gate, turned and slowed.

VISITS TO PLACES

Then it was for the place alone
I was there. It was not the barrow,
Nor the legendary smith who shod horses,
It was the contained and held singularity
Of the place itself.

There was a breathing oneness
Which had always been there.
I imagined our ancestors choosing –
'Here we shall bury our dead', and understood.
Here, where the veil is thin, here,
Where the spirit-world batters against
Numbed human sensitivities,
Momentarily piercing our autism.
Here.

~ Grace Blindell

Chanonry Point

Standing upon wet sand
Round flat pebbles
Graced with vision –

Unbelievable pod of Dolphin –
Out from their own wet world –
A curvaceous surge

Out from Avoch
   To Rosemarkie:

Sharp prints of boots in sand
Precariously etched
Hard plod along a wet strand
Overhead cloud and
Moray Firth choppy
Far-off houses remain far-off

Abruptly all languor lifts
Look!
And another!
And again and again!

Shape of dolphin leaping
Clean clear of all doubt
Grey curve of living light.

~ Richard Meyers

Song for Semerwater

Your glassy surface reflects the hills around you;
moorland, pasture and a fringe of trees along your margin
meet themselves at your waters' edge.
Above, curlews wind up their cries in trilling crescendo
lapwings call 'pee-witt' across the valley.
Florescent green moss blankets walls and branches.
I watch Canada geese float across your water
gaggling in comfortable conversation,
while other waterfowl twit and squawk among the reeds.
Two oyster-catchers fly over the lake
their voices ring ping-ping in chorus,
and four brown geese travel to another nesting ground.

We have squelched through thick mud to get here.
Now we clamber down to your shore,
wash our wellies in the clear water
and return along the pebble beach.
A breeze has sprung up, ruffling your surface,
the sky is grey as we head for home,
carrying the echoes of your song
for future remembering.

~ Joan Angus

Lifestyle

4

LIFESTYLE

Celtic Blessing
Written at a GreenSpirit annual gathering writing workshop

May the spirit of Nantlle be with you,
This Autumn day.

May the flow of stream be with you,
Passing obstacles on its way,
And falling into the ever present lake.

May the decay of quarry be with you,
Crumbling its old, worn structures,.
Into the holding Earth.

May the magic of myth be with you,
Transforming all that is within,
Into an alchemy of gold.

May the strength of the hills hold you,
Through sun and rain, wind and storm,
Until you are ready to tread your path again.

And may you feel the presence of all of the Earth around you.
Brightness of sun.
Silence of moon,
Breath of trees,
This day,
Until your journeys end.

~ Ian Mowll

Final Prayer

Star of morning
Star of evening
Streets and strangers
View to the world
Outside
Now and the hour when
Our leaving will be
Our arriving
Axure star
Star of gold
Point the way
Be with us
Welcome us
Blue star of lapis
Star of amethyst
Mother that birthed
Wrens and rivers
Pray for
Us all now and
At the start
Of our return
Amen

~ Richard Meyers

LIFESTYLE

Where the mind is without fear…

and the head is held high
Where knowledge is free
Where the world has not been broken up into fragments
By narrow domestic walls
Where words come from the depth of truth
Where tireless striving stretches its arms towards perfection
Where the clear stream of reason has not lost its way
Into the dreary desert sand of dead habit
Where the mind is led forward by thee
Into ever-widening thought and action
Into that heaven of freedom, my Father, let my country awake

~ Rabindranath Tagore

Hold Fast to that which is Good

Let me be open to all that is good
and not drown in the ugliness of this world.
Let me be mindful of those silken moments
when the senses awaken to beauty,
moments that strike chords of delight,
that cause the flagging spirit to soar.
Let me be mindful of the love in the world:
at this very moment people are embracing each other,
endearments are being spoken,
right now acts of loving kindness are taking place.
As I watch,
sociable sparrows splash in the bird bath
and my companion enters the room with a smile.

~ Peter Watkins

*   *   *

Sung at gatherings before each meal

From the Earth the grain,
the gift of life to feed us.
From the sky the rain,
bring blessings on our bread.
Earth and water, fire and air,
the gift of life to feed us.
Earth and water, fire and air,
bring blessings on our bread.

~ Alan Whear and Jenny Joyce

LIFESTYLE

A Daily Jubilation

The morning sun
has crept over the eastern horizon,
eased in through the curtains,
entered my closed eyes
and stirred me from sleep.

A robin is perched on the garden table
looking in at me looking out.
The bird feeders are already busy.
Starlings muscle in,
goldfinches flit,
greenfinches wait,
blue tits swing acrobatically
and the jubilant house sparrows chirrup on the fence.

If a poem can be a prayer
I want it to give thanks for the ordinary miracles of life.
To wake, to be greeted by these feathered beings is a daily gift.
What would the world be without birdsong?

I put on a coat
and go out to greet the sparrows:
Hello my friends –
Morning to you my cheerful companions.
How can I be downcast
when all my garden birds are saying:
This is another God given day – live,
live heartfully.

~ Peter Watkins

glory be to Gaia

glory be to Gaia,
for rainbows, glaciers and fresh snow;
we honour and praise you, Gaia,
mysterious blue planet
unique in this vast universe;
like your widest rivers our hearts
flow with gratitude.
    glory be to Gaia
    for forests, valleys and exquisite flowers;
    we honour and praise you, Gaia,
    great mother,
    thank you for clean air and water,
    and all the fruits and seeds
    manifest through your abundant power.
glory be to Gaia,
for birdsong, mountains and clear lakes;
we honour and praise you, Gaia,
giant pulsating orb of life
from which we've grown –

LIFESTYLE

please help us feel our interdependence
with all animal and human kin.
  glory be to Gaia,
  for millipedes, worms and all tiny creatures;
  we honour and praise you, Gaia,
  ceaseless wheel of life,
  we embrace your eternal cycle,
  the rich soil our bodies will become,
  and the gift this present moment is.
glory be to Gaia,
for whales, phosphorescence and fish;
we honour and praise you, Gaia,
planet-jewel of the cosmos,
sacred being infused in our dna;
please light the spark of peace in us
that we may serve this precious life.

~ Helen Moore

Thou Great Source of All
Whose breath is the daily genesis of life,
You, who are both the mysterious energy that sustains the universe,
And also that invisible attraction we call gravity –
Holding all that is in a compassionate embrace,
May the miracle of our own being fill us with awe and wonder.

Great Spirit, whose exuberant benevolence we see all around,
In the sweet scented herbs and the earthy potato,
In the crisp juiciness of the apple and the generous grain,
Release us from meanness and fear,
May we partake of our food with mindfulness and gratitude –

Deep Wisdom, for whom creation is both continuous and circular,
May we learn from the fallen tree –
Dead, yet bringing forth new life –
Lift from us the gnawing fear of our own death.
Give us instead that deeper understanding and trust
That we may see beyond our own individual cessation
To a wider and more wonderful continuation.

LIFESTYLE

Spirit, whose being contains all opposites,
Tenderly hold us – who embody within ourselves
That same paradox of dark and light, of pain and joy,
That we may be brought to a balanced whole –

Oh Thou Nameless One who are truly beyond our comprehension
Yet within whom we live and move and have our being,
Our prayer is that our vision may be widened,
That our self-imposed restraints be loosened
That we may become that which we truly are –
Each one of us an expression of that wild and magnificent creativity
Which pours itself out in never – ending abundance –

~ Grace Blindell

What I Would Do

Connect to what enfolds us
Be moved by this world's beauty
Be outraged by the cruelty and the
Despoiling of our earth
Know that I have a place here
Though often afraid and full of doubt
Arrogant and prickly
Loving words and music
Being an empty vessel
Chants, prayers and meditation
Woods and wild places
Read poetry in word and what
Flies and slithers and sings
Listen out for fox calls
Don't take the stars for granted
Nor leaf shape nor rainfall nor

LIFESTYLE

The arm that encircles you nor
That person's breath by your ear.

For God's sake don't spend all day
By the laptop
Turn the damn thing off
Get out and taste the morning
Complete your poem
Go out and meet your friend
As Rumi says
"You've got a body
don't act as though you haven't
go out and
walk in the rain."

~ Richard Meyers

S.A.D.

O Mother Gaia, remind me to enjoy the small things in life:
To marvel at the perfection of the last flowers of summer,
    amidst the autumn debris;
To be cheered by the robin's bright plumage against the gloom
    of winter;
To be excited at the sight of a rainbow in the midst of a stormy sky.

O Mother Gaia, show me the positive in every situation:
The gifts of sight, smell and hearing amidst the fear of ill health
    and ageing;
The love and companionship of a partner by my side against
    the fear of loneliness;
The fun amidst the hum drum routine.

O Mother Gaia, teach me how to live, laugh and love;
To see the good in all things living;
To see the funny side;
To be joyful!

~ Joan Angus

LIFESTYLE

Two Poems about Time:

Wasting time

is not time wasted
but time gathered
    into the circle
    of quiet where
    the quiet comes
    alive. It's full of music
    that sings in the soul
    and harmonises
    with the poem in the heart
    and the turning of the Earth

Time

    Could you and I
Turn ourselves around?
  Could we turn to live,
    not by a ticking clock
or bossy digital numbers,
    but by time moved
as a tall tree moves
    in a small wind, time
told by awareness of sun,
    moon, the long breath
      of a redwood over
      a millennium.

~ Kay McMullen SNDdeN

Don't Let the Normals Get You

Don't let the normals get you,
They will sanitise you,
and cleanse you of your passion.
Don't let the normals get you,
They will stop you wearing outrageous clothes,
in the name of convention.
Don't let the normals get you,
They will make your friendships and relationships plain vanilla,
and not allow for trouble and spice.
Don't let the normals get you,
They will put you into a plastic house,
Away from the wildness of nature.
Don't let the normals get you,
They will make you live with the status quo,
And not let you dream of a better world.

~ Ian Mowll

LIFESTYLE

Metaphorical Memo to Myself

Stop walking the clean straight roads only
Seek our curving course mucky by-ways
Ignore all neatly aligned 3 by 3 slabs
The verge has much more to offer –
Hedgerow harvests
Blackberries, wild damsons, hazelnuts
Bite occasional frost dusted sloes
Thrill of a taste brazen abrasive
When you run out of words –
Stop talking
Keep walking
Descend steep inclines at a run
Pole vault over ditches
Sing more
Laugh often
Dance.

~ Richard Meyers

Eco Crone

You might call mine a draughty house. I call it a house that
 breathes.
You might call it an unswept home. I call it shared territory;
 people and spiders live here.
You might call it a messy garden. I call it Permaculture.
You might chide me for not netting my blackcurrants,
 strawberries, loganberries …
I say these are not my fruits. They are our fruits. Everyone who
 lives here, shares; blackbirds, people, what's the difference? We
 all like fruit.

You might think I'm strange to prefer birdsong over CDs, bird
 table antics, (and the parade of flowers and the never-ending
 pageant of the sky) over TV.
No. I don't miss the digitized spectacle of antelopes or Antarctic
 penguins.
I live here, half way down a country hill, with robins on my
 windowsill.
And laundry flapping on the line. I love the sights and sounds and
 smells of here.
Logs burn to keep me warm.
Here I snuggle close to the Earth as I can get and still be a
 householder.

Sometimes I overlook those big, Celtic moments – solstices,
 equinoxes –
and celebrate instead, morning after morning,

LIFESTYLE

The tiny moments, tiny movements, tiny changes in the hedgerow.
I rejoice with the first snowdrop, I mourn the dead badger by the
    roadside, I tremble and shudder as the sparrowhawk plunges
    for the kill and I know I must say yes to that.
I bless the food I grew – or someone else grew, not too far from
    here –
and I ask forgiveness for the miles it took to bring to my cool,
    climatic zone the rice, the spice, the oranges and the fair trade
    bananas.
I sing songs of my own invention
and converse with my teachers, the trees, who teach me how to live
    in the Now.

Whenever I have to move
into the plastic world of corporations, shopping malls and cars and
    planes,
I reach for a talisman: the moss on the sidewalk's edge, a paving
    stone
dislodged by the determination of a plane tree's roots, pigeons in
    the park,
a smile on the face of the Mexican woman who cleans the motel
    room,
the splendid upper surfaces of clouds. Something to keep me
    tethered,
keep me connected to my spiritual source.

I walk always in flat shoes, and barefoot when I can.
I love the sun's rays on my skin.
I love this body that made miracles – new life, warm milk.

And now I love it in its quietness.
I celebrate my shrinking, my wrinkling, my aging,
the slow arc of my journey from the soil back to the soil.
I want to use this body up, every breath, every drop of blood, wear it out,
till all that's left is a small, dry husk, dancing in the wind …

~ Marian Van Eyk Mc Cain

* * *

Walk Softly
Based on Chung Hyun Kyung

Walk softly on the Earth
Massage her with your feet
Because when you are walking
You walk on your Mother's face

~ June Boyce Tillman

Relationships

5

RELATIONSHIPS

Friendship

Oh, the comfort,
The inexpressible comfort,
Of feeling safe with a person;
Having neither to weigh thoughts nor measure words,
But pour them all out, just as they are –
Chaff and grain together,
Knowing that a faithful hand
Will take and sift them,
Keep what is worth keeping,
And then with the breath of kindness
Blow the rest away.

~ George Eliot

Double Digging

Double digging the vegetable plot, just as you taught me;
A rhythm of movement, turning the soil into the advanced trench.
Slice – stoop – lift – slice – stoop – lift,
The clean sound of steel slicing through the giving soil,
The sweet moist smell of the turned earth after rain.

And what were you thinking
As you watched me inexpertly dig your garden?
That ritual turning, a kind of succession.
Did you quietly rage at your frailty?

We were close in those moments
And I wish we could have said more.

But perhaps each crumbling clod of earth was word enough
Slice – stoop – lift – slice – stop – lift
Digging too, can be an act of love.

~ Peter Watkins
For my father Albert Henry Watkins (1907–1983)

RELATIONSHIPS

Friends

We are as spirits met as one,
As minds which claim a common interest
As hearts which share in friendship's greatest prize,
An honest linking in each other's eyes.

~ Christine Roe

*   *   *

Dancing

I reach out a hand,
it is taken.
I take a step
I am led.
I hear music,
I move to the rhythm
hand in hand
step by step
never alone.
Feeling the beat
in the soles of our feet
the dance of life
leads us on.

~ Sarah Jane Toleman

Ode to a Pair of Walking Boots

Look at you now,
moving slowly, over damp leaves.
Mud-splashed, shabby,
parting at the welt,
incontinent.
Could you do it all again?
Walk the Grand Canyon north to south?
Stride. Through dust and stones. Yucca. Snow. White rock,
red rock, Ayers Rock.
That smooth-backed stone whale stranded at the heart
of a hard and hard-baked land of rock and sand.
Do you remember
the screech of cockatoos, relentless dry,
heat, leaves dried to a crisp?
Or would you rather
think of the bayou, and wet, polished knees of swamp
cypresses? Mist rising from still water
and the silent watching eyes of alligators?
Leeches have crept
their strange, swift, ghastly head-toe, head-toe
measure across you – till I screamed. And flicked them off.
Yet you were uperturbed.

RELATIONSHIPS

Do you recall
that ancient aesclepion
we travelled miles to see, through
olive and carob? Greek goats browsing
half up, half down the wizened, leaning trees. And where,
when we had waited long
beside the crystal water,
you, patient on grey pebbles, till my toes
had finished flirting with the sun, the old woman let us in.
I was ashamed of you,
standing there, so large and crass
Upon those delicate
thousand-year old tiles.
I do apologise.
For I'm so proud of you.
That's why you are still here, now,
with me, in this green valley where we live
our quiet days. We reminisce
under the oak and beech
in our old age, yours and mine.
And here we'll stay, the three of us.
Until it is time, dear, loyal friends
for the recycling
of your well-worn, well-faded leather,
and my own.

~ Marian Van Eyk McCain

Whales Weep Not!

They say the sea is cold, but the sea contains
the hottest blood of all, and the wildest, the most urgent.

All the whales in the wider deeps, hot are they, as they urge
on and on, and dive beneath the icebergs.
The right whales, the sperm whales, the hammer heads, the killers
there they blow, there they blow, hot white wild breath out of
    the sea!

And they rock, and they rock, through the sensual ageless ages
on the depths of the seven seas,
and through the salt they reel with drunk delight
and in the tropics tremble they with love
and roll with massive, strong desire, like gods.
Then the great bull lies up against his bride
in the blue deep bed of the sea,
as mountain pressing on mountain, in the zest of life:
and out of the inward roaring of the inner red ocean of
    whale-blood
the long tip reaches strong, intense, like the maelstrom-tip and
    comes to rest
in the clasp and the soft, wild clutch of a she-whale's fathomless
    body.

RELATIONSHIPS

And over the bridge of the whale's strong phallus, linking the
    wonder of whales
the burning archangels under the sea keep passing, back and forth,
keep passing, archangels of bliss
from him to her, from her to him, great Cherubim
that wait on whales in mid-ocean, suspended in the waves of
    the sea
great heaven of whales in the waters, old hierarchies.

And enormous mother whales lie dreaming suckling their
    whale-tender young
and dreaming with strange whale eyes wide open in the waters of
    the beginning and the end.
And bull-whales gather their women and whale calves in a ring
when danger threatens, on the surface of the ceaseless flood
and range themselves like great fierce Seraphim facing the threat
encircling their huddled monsters of love.
And all this happens in the sea, in the salt
where God is also love, but without words:
and Aphrodite is the wife of whales
most happy, happy she!

and Venus among the fishes skips and is a she-dolphin
she is the gay, delighted porpoise sporting with love and the sea
she is the female tunny-fish, round and happy among the whales
and dense with happy blood, dark rainbow bliss in the sea.

~ DH Lawrence

That Most Precious Greeting

I want to say how are you and mean it;
As if I'd said:
Talk to me of your sorrows and I will tell you mine.
I never want that most precious greeting
to become a throw away line.

Do we not have griefs to share?
Do we not all yearn for intimacy?
And yet
We live as if suffering were
a weakness, an indulgence we can't allow.
Move on
Get on with living is
the favoured maxim now.

How are you?

Can't complain!

~ Peter Watkins

RELATIONSHIPS

Dance of the Spirit

In darkness
I reach out my hand;
it is taken.
I feel a breath on my cheek,
The pull of my heart;
I listen.
I do not know
the road
but I know my hand
is held.
I am never alone;
my heart hears your call.

I journey on
with joy and hope;
trusting.
I push away
my need to see,
my want for surety.
Your way may be a mystery
but there is freedom
in letting myself go.

~ Sarah Jane Toleman

Grandmother

Her hands
bore flat, brown freckles, and a golden ring.
Her lap was a walled garden,
fragrant with lavender,
humming with bees,
as she hummed
her comfort songs in my small ears,
and her breath dried
my tears.
Those years
held home-baked bread and elderberry wine,
the quiet ticking of a mantel clock,
and evenings when we sat
around a real hearth to tell real tales.
Back then, the only thing
that brought us flickering pictures was the fire,
in front of which
the dogs and cats lay sleeping,
folded together on a worn, brown mat.

RELATIONSHIPS

Those far-off days lie warm, like that,
in my heart space.
Now, my hands
bear flat, brown freckles and a golden ring,
and I can comfort too, and bake, and sing.
But there is more
to do – if I can dare
to go beyond the garden wall, into
an unfamiliar field.
And sing my song
out loud, and sure and strong, until
the weeping Earth is healed.

~ Marian Van Eyk McCain

Faith That

In the blistering heat
A cool spring may be found

That after a painful night
There will be a morning respite

Though your hand has left mine
I will again feel your touch

That love will at last return
The stranger recognised and made welcome

That simple joy will be felt and
A child's laughter and mirth
Fall like moisture to the parched land

Faith
that we are held as we stumble
Freefalling
Not like stones but lightly
As feathers down to welcoming ground.

~ Richard Meyers

Seasons

6

SEASONS

Harvest Poem

Harvest is a food crop
A time of gathering
A moment of recollection
A blackberry eaten
    With full attention
Potatoes placed in a bucket
Runner beans overflowing a bowl
Strawberries piled high – a sprinkling
Of sugar, cream from a china jug
Harvest is a recollection
It is a child's laughter
It is finding myself anew
Amid the briars
Fingers purple stained
It is apple and blackberry crumble
It is peering into a still pool
And seeing our voices echo
It is the birth of a child
It is the night sky
It is love
It is given
It is gift.

~ Richard Meyers

This Much I Know

It is autumn.
In the garden everything has lost its lustre.
Sunflowers bend their petal heads towards the earth,
I want to say, in supplication.
This happens every year and each time is a kind of loss.
I urge them, stay – stay longer, just as you are,
but oh no they say, no we cannot stay,
we are part of something bigger and more glorious by far.

Everything is impermanent;
you, me, the hawthorn tree,
the running hare,
the robin with its winter song. And
although we might think that
we endure full long,
with the sunflowers I agree,
our little lives surely are
but a brief showing and
part of something much bigger
and more glorious by far.

~ Peter Watkins

Samhain New Moon

Here in my hand,
an absolute beginning place. The seed of a flower
that will blossom in the Springtime. The earth,
on my fingertips,

the wind passing through,
the wet of the rain,
blowing over. This night is the deepest of deep,
and in the darkness, my heart opens.

Many days ago, the full moon
slipped over horizons
shaping a future in the sky and
shadows on the sea.

And now we are here, embracing potential in the dark,
with the waves beckoning me home; the ocean,
and my heart, a wide horizon.

~ Bryony Rogers

Temporary Arrangements

I kneel and plant the fallen conker,
Still as death it lies
A stillness of unbeing
In the coagulated winter soil.

Yet within that blackened shell,
That dense and hardened flesh
Flickers an unease –
A whisper of memory stirs within its clenched and clodded self.

It is the dance, it is the rhythm,
It is the magic alchemy
Which stirs and calls forth struggle.
The conker obeying its habitual path,
Dow and up, root and shoot,
A chestnut tree is born.

And yet…
The chestnut tree and I are both
Temporary arrangements.

Morphic resonance whispers memory of being,
Whispers pattern but never permanence
Patterns arise, blend and fade,
The dance shifts and changes,
Intention co-exists with impermanence.

The chestnut tree and I
Are both temporary arrangements.

Yet every seven years or so
I am remade with different stuff,
And what was me…
becomes (perhaps) the chestnut tree,
Temporarily.

~ Grace Blindell

Leaves

From the late autumn on
through winter days and nights, and into March,
they huddle by the mat.
Brown-skinned refugees
pressed close against the door, waiting a chance.
And when it comes, they ride
the sudden, welcome breeze of opportunity.
Weightless, on crinkled edges, light and swift,
through in an instant, dodging the sentry broom
with rustling laughter,
dancing with delight across the flagstones,
swirling into the hallway,
they seek asylum
at the bottom of the stairs.
Now if you think it strange that I should care
to leave them there – such outside things inside –
then you should know:
this is my passport back to times
when I and mine
lived deep within the land's stone lap;
back to the days
when man and mammoth shared a creaturehood,
when babies lay on skins,
and smoky fires of wood were all we had to light the night.

SEASONS

Those were the days
when inside blurred with outside at an edge
forever indistinct.
Back then,
there was no doormat. And there were no doors
to keep us in – or out.
No walls to separate
us from each other, or from Her,
the Mother of us all,
the tree of life from whom all leaves and people fall.

~ Marian Van Eyk McCain

Rain – A View Through a Window

It is a grey rain filled autumn day.
Rain raps
Like a thousand finger nails on the window pain.
Motile droplets course down the glass,
alive and shining in what light there is.
Trees shake their yellow-leafed branches
as if in celebration and drink it in.
Newly ploughed and planted,
the glad fields lie naked and receive it as a gift.
A bedraggled blackbird
shelters low in the blackthorn hedge
waiting for earthworms
surfacing after the rain.

I want to be out in the gloom of the day,
feel the cold replenishing rain on my skin,
feel the wind tug at my clothes,
doing nothing but walking
the lost lanes
alive and shining in what light there is.

~ Peter Watkins

SEASONS

Letting Dark Be Dark

The voices kept insisting,
"Make up your mind
Now
Find an answer
Now
Indecision is weakness
Not knowing is a dumb game."

But there was a new voice which whispered…
"Wait,
Stay in the darkness,
It will enclose you as velvet.
Embrace the pain,
For it is a necessity of new birth.

And do not reject 'not knowing'
For to stand quietly with
Uncertainty
Is both trust and wisdom.
The answer will come,
But in its own time,
Not yours."

~ Grace Blindell

Winter Solstice – Dark Night Ensouled

On this night-day
crisp-sharp-darkness secrets dreaming

Earth still, wind gasping for breath
Fire, withholding its very light-being
Flickering embers – don't warm cold dry bones

This deep deep black satin
Itself only transient – mortal

We turn once more
Pathway our pilgrim age
Encircling the glowing ember
Solstice to solstice

What dream awakens?
Here – now?
Out with the old – borne with the new?
Yule and Christ-mass entwined

~ Chris Newsam

SEASONS

A poem for Winter Solstice

If you look for it

Among the gloom you will see a light.
Among the fear and despondency you will find a hand to hold.
Among the pain and grief there will be comfort.
Among the loneliness there is love.
Among the conflict there are pockets of peace.

Amidst death and decay there is life stirring.
Amidst the dark of the night there are stars shining.

Open your eyes,
Look, you can see it now.
Come closer, turn away from your troubles.
Hope rises with the dawning of a new year.

~ Joan Angus

Hoorah for the snow!

Oh! horror of horrors,
those light fluffy flakes
drifting down from the sky
will disrupt our structured lives

cars are stuck
buses don't run
the post doesn't come
and everyone is walking!

We grab shovels and spades
and work
with our neighbours
for freedom.

But the snow turns to ice
and we slip and we slide
then decide
to take the kids sledging instead.

We wade to the tops of our wellies.
The air fills with snowballs and laughter
The children walk to school!

Under the snow hidden treasures grow.
The wheel of the seasons is turning.
The warmth of the earth will bring new birth
and hope will emerge from our yearning.

~ Joan Angus

SEASONS

Snowfall and the Cold

Each flake askance
Every-which-way
Ground thick
With whiteness:

Pity the homeless
Even our inside walls
Are damp-cold – unforgiving
Many die in doorways.

Take a can opener
To your cold heart
Rich man and
God bless you Sir!

~ Richard Meyers

Forest Walk

We pace the space.
Foot falls silent.
Trees stand tall and still.
Heather bushes to the edges
of the track.

Old roots creep underfoot:
push up stones.
Earth lies cool and damp
after nurturing rains.
All holds breath.

Deep down roots search:
drink in the richness.
Seeds stir:
Shift root and shoot to
seek depth and light.

SEASONS

Sunlight draws
all living things
towards the warmth.
Birds sing.
Insects get busy

We drink it in,
Along with the
taut, wound up,
about to burst
energy
of spring.

~ Sarah Jane Toleman

Winter Solstice

The darkness has come,
wrapping us round, taking us further
inside. It has been gradual steps, day
by day, night by night, hour by hour, the darkness
lengthening. It comes,

this great shawl of winter, promising
a secret, a deep knowing,
the remembering of the silence
we were born to.

We inhale. Empty
ourselves out, and light

a candle
for the sun's return. Begin
again.

~ Bryony Rogers

River in Winter

Ice, like the demure edging of petticoats
Laces the river.
Fragile tracery, delicate, cold.
There, where the rocks protrude, and here
Where innocent branches dip and bob,
The tiny uneven transparent frills
Stiff, like frou-frous, hand-cuff their victims.
At night the crewel bobbins fly
Pricking out the pattern on congealed water,
Pinning it down. Its laughing dancing life stilled.

Rigor mortis of rivers.

See, it is where the river loved most
That the pain begins.
Round the smoothed rocks, the oft-kissed twigs,
The gently lapped sides.

Yet... without this winter...
No spring.

~ Grace Blindell

Springtime with Amida

Sun hiding behind cloud cover
Bright star screened by trees

All around our little woodland
Snowdrops have arisen and crocus

Tongues grass green have pushed
Free of last year's leaves a –

Tender savagery of spears
Below the garden hedge

What imbues this growing?
What inner knowing?

What whispered word
Subtly uttered calls?

And as the egg is laid within the
Spiralling of leaves
And grass and moss –

What is it that taps and taps
From the inside looking to emerge
Out into the light?

~ Richard Meyers

The Music of April's Stillness

There is a stillness deepdown things today

I can nearly hear the worms' journeyings
and the wriggling of the tardigrades in the water butt

The curving edges of the skyclouds are no longer straitened by
crosslines
and the fountain burbles an undertone

The falling catkins noiselessly pattern the sunmottled lawn
and the scrabble of the squirrels offers a tooloud rattle
in the pianissimo symphony

The burgeoning green leaves
Will soon be big enough to rustle

Finely tuned branches
perform a graceful dance of varying rhythms
over the bench on which I sit.

All is at rest.

And I long to join.

~ June Boyce Tillman

NOTE: Tardigrades are very small creatures. They are never more than 1.5 mm
long, and can only be seen with a microscope.

My Life as a Wave

a shadow of the ocean breaker
I was not so long ago

I've travelled the whole Atlantic
to rest on this particular shell-white strand
under an April full moon

in my lips I've caught mussels
and pearls, slow scuttlings of crabs
green and maroon wigs of weed

I've caught panickings of fish
still blue keenings of porpoise
the ghosts of herring

I've caught a shoal of silence

SEASONS

out there in the deep sea
where sailboats and gannets wing
where we're unruffled into one long fathomless body

I breathe, in and out

no end to the cycle of tides
no end to the I that is we
our deep song

and still I break
still I break
I break

~ Roselle Anguin

Petals Falling

Cast off by swelling fruits
the clothing of youth falls fluttering.
Baby buds of spring have had their day
all too briefly.
Scented blossoms in their delightful profusion
are just a memory.

Now we watch and wait.
Seeds of dreams and ambitions
have yet to mature
while the seasons come and go.
Through passionate summer storms
and soft, sunny days
the fruit swells
nurtured by life's experience.

Until in autumn's fiery glory
the fruits are ready to gather
each one a treasure in its juicy fullness.
We celebrate abundance.

And from each fruit, flesh devoured, a seed
potential for future trees
a hundred-fold.
Life renews itself

~ Joan Angus

Chiaroscuro

The moment July is in the ascendant,
an assortment of sky-lit tenants
needs to be hypnotised by the heat.

In the iced blues of January,
south-facing windows permit slanting sun
to investigate much closer to the ground...
It alights on every cheekbone and pin.

Walking south-east along a three o'clock street,
those who once longed for the prime red-yellows of July
are quite astounded at themselves – at how soundly they are
absorbed
into that shadow play, that chiaroscuro.

~ Jenny Johnson

First published in Sarasvati

Note. Chiaroscuro is the use of strong contrasts between light and dark.

Faith

Is this what they call faith:
believing that one day there will be light
coming again into this shrouded place,
this slow, dark river at the bottom of a sunless cave
where blind fish swim ?
Is this what they call faith:
believing that before long there will be
a stirring in the deep, black water,
of something small, more smelled and felt than seen,
like the knowing of Spring that comes before
the snowdrops bloom ?
A promise
like a tiny, faintly flickering lamp, held by a messenger who
rides before the dawn.
A turning
that happens when the pendulum of night
reaches its farthest stretch and pauses,
rests for a heartbeat in between
the breathing out and breathing in.
This is the oyster's hinge,
opening, closing with the rhythms of the tide.
This is the waltz of life, the tiptoe pause before the glide.
Loosen your fingers, now, from the dark rocks.
Be ready. For the tide is turning. Soon
there will be light. Quite soon, there will be light.
You cannot see it yet, but it will come. Believe it will – and
must.
They call this faith.

~ Marian Van Eyk McCain

Meetings with Nature's Community

7

It Can Be Explained

It can be explained, the gift of flight;
the anatomy, the physiology
the aerodynamics.
So too, the mystery of migrations,
courtship displays, nesting habits, even song,
are all revealed by scientific investigations.

But is it behind the knowing,
that makes the spirit swell
in joy and reverential wonder
at the aerial acrobatics of swallows as they fly
or the song of the invisible lark
held in a brilliant blue sky?

~ Peter Watkins

Trees

If you asked what trees are
people would tell you
in their proudest voices

trees are great beings
who are often lonely
company is all they want
for their souls are sometimes gaunt
because they will always be bound
to the earth, the ground

many of them are cheerful things though
and you should say hello
you don't have to say it out loud
they are clever things you know

when they are together
they chatter and whistle all night
but they will never fight
their gnarled fingers scraping at the sky
trying to leave the earth and fly

MEETINGS WITH NATURE'S COMMUNITY

the mighty oak, leader of them all
the weeping willow, whose tentacles do fall
the great pine hailing down spikes
and the beautiful juniper that nobody dislikes

so if you ever feel alone
talk to the trees and they will moan
with joy to be noticed
if you listen carefully they will talk
they will listen to you like a hawk
then you will have an eternal friend

*Based on a poem called The Dancing Disk in the Sky
by Hibaq Osman.*

~ Ellis Mortimer, aged 11years

Tree Meets Me

Robin speak to me of Oak
Tell me her name
Is it growth, the how of her
Is it love, the why of her
Is it now, the where of her.

Oak speak to me of Robin
Why does he move me so.
His song rings through your arms
And rings through me.
He is an echo from your past
He is a siren to your future
He is singing now.

Why do you shine so
with your patterned trunk,
lifting up the moss and
growing your world.
A community of beings rest in you
A galaxy is born because of you.

~ Nigel Lees

Mother Nature's Dance

Beauty of the morning dew
that falls as silently as droplet dust
refreshing every inch of grass
and every throbbing cut and thrust.
The birds they sing their songs for us:
the echo of the cuckoo's call, the trilling wren,
the warbling finch,
from mountain top to flooded fen.
The trees, they tilt their heads to us
the faeries whisper greeting as we pass
and spiders weave their tangled worlds
of shining, silken thread.
You are my world, my looking glass
my song, my shelter from the storm,
you teach in every knowing glance
and every trembling kiss
the awesomeness of formless form
and Mother Nature's dance.

~ David Kelf

A Feeling from Childhood

When I played in the stream in the woods as a child,
and plunged my legs up to my thighs in its soft clay mud,
and baked them dry beneath in the sunlight,
lying on my back on the bank and watching the clouds sail by
    above,
I merged a little with the Earth.
And when I made for myself garlands of ivy
and climbed a tree to the highest point that would bear my weight,
listening to the mysteries whispered by the rustling leaves,
then I forgot for a while which was tree and which was I.
And when I touched the pink ragged robin
that grew by the edge of the marsh,
I felt that I touched the garment of the Universe
and my fingers tingled with the softness and the beauty of it.

~ Vivianne Crowley

Gull Dawn

Long after I have left
I will remember the gulls
carrying dawn to me,

the ragged wires of their voices
slowly skewering my dreams open.
I am tuned to that sound

of something calling its name over and over
bringing themselves back
into bone, beak, wings, claws
as they fly out of their dark roost
here they come across
the dragontail of rock

as the sky flushes open,
calling the sun up over the horizon.

~ Sue Proffitt

Cormorant

The cormorant over the river
Is doing its 'angel act'.
Holding its wings protective
Over the sad old world.

I saw one yesterday too
On the beach.
Solitary and still, its wings spread wide,
How serious and intent its ritual.

Some say it dries its wings,
Others it cools itself,
But I think otherwise –
For I at least feel blessed,
Feel more protected – understood
Because of the cormorant doing its 'angel act'.

~ Grace Blindell

Sandpipers

The tiny sandpipers
Look like embryonic seraphim
Awaiting their ascension into heaven

Keeping themselves busy meanwhile
By running at top speed
Through wet sand.

Thus practising for when
As bright messengers of truth
They will travel much faster than light.

~ Grace Blindell

Swallows

Every April
they arrive
those Olympians of the air,
journeying from South Africa
across desert, mountain, sea;
their navigational aid
set to a barn in Suffolk
where they raise their young in mud cups
and wheel and skim about the fields
in an ecstasy of flight

And I almost want to sing out a hymn of gratitude.
I want to greet them like exotic neighbours,
which they are
returned home after a long winter's absence.

~ Peter Watkins

Oystercatcher

You shed your crab-shell orange bill, its slender length
still attached to the seashell whorls of skull; such fragile casing
for the powerhouse whose songlines map the shore.

What would it be if I could unmake your death, repatriate
your bones, ravel backwards through the slow decay
of sinew, muscle, flesh; see you lift off the tideline

in your raiments of black and white, plumage slicked
and faithful to the needs of water, strand and air; feel your flicker
of daisychain pulse, the rush of blood through every cell;

witness the dance of particle and wave that animates your eye;
spool right back to that depression in the sand where,
in an egg the size of your adult cranium, the moment

of inspiration started with the first bright meteorite
of consciousness, became the fluid haunting stream
that's oystercatcher song, your bright *I am*.

~ Roselle Anguin

Butterfly

She flutters down to a tasty leaf
and lays her minute egg
to stand on its base
like a tiny yellow pot
packed full of promise.

Inside, warmed by the sun,
a caterpillar takes shape
and grows. The eggshell breaks,
he spills out onto the leaf,
caterpillars to the edge
and eats and grows.

The days and nights grow cold.
Caterpillar spins silk
to wrap himself a cocoon
which hardens to become a shell.
He falls to the ground.

MEETINGS WITH NATURE'S COMMUNITY

Protected by autumn leaves,
inside the chrysalis
a miracle happens:
caterpillar becomes soup
then a living creature
waiting for the sun.

The shell splits
legs…head…wings
magically unfurl
to become
an exact replica of its parent.

Wings, covered in tiny coloured scales
shimmer in the light breeze
and flutter away.

A new life has been born
out of death and destruction
a metaphor of spirit.

~ Joan Angus

Bat-Being

When the small upside-down being
With the big ears and the radar
Follows its inbuilt pattern
To be Bat... then
The secret and introvert darkness
Is suddenly criss-crossed with signals.
They tremble in the air
Vibrating hidden harmonics,
Zapping the cold dank walls.

There emerges then a form of aliveness
Both subtle and arcane,
Quite beyond the comprehension
Of the brash and flashy dwellers of daylight.

~ Grace Blindell

Spider's Web

New day
She feeds it in her silk body
Round and round
Trillions of spirals
Down the years
In my window frame
First the spokes
Then the rigging
Tailored to ensnare
Flies, wasps and moths
Open weaved blind
Dew jeweled sparkling
Early autumn
Morning
New day.

~ Richard Meyers

Slowworm

A celtic brooch
Moulds itself to
Grassy contours
Silver grey
Muscled lace
Gleams glints
Mid-morning sun
Bright tiny eyes

~ Richard Meyers

Cobwebs

I like the way cobwebs
straddle a room
insinuating curves
across an angular ceiling,
defying gravity and
insisting their existence
out of reach.
Dieting spiders whom I rarely see
have a peck of fly
occasionally
but really seem to dine
on nothing but time.
Methinks I have no right
to bring them down to earth
floored by a broom.
Let them trapeze their life aloft
while scrape by below.

~Miranda Cox

Dandelion

The sun's face shines
in yours.
The lion's mane
is not as bright
or glamorous.
Your toothed leaves
crouch in the grass
waiting.

You open as the sun rises
and shut at its setting.
At your final closing
your petals transform.
At break of day
your golden face
is replaced
by an old frosted head.

The breeze gently
breathes on
your silver globe
causing a silent soft
explosion.
Hundreds of your dancing
children
float up into the blue.

Some are caught
in the damp grass
or in cobwebs
where they hang,
strung between stalks:
a row of bobbing stars
which when released
grow rampant in the garden.

~ Sarah Jane Toleman

Nightfall

When all was dark and coldly still, the wind
With stealth rose to his feet and stretched
His mighty wings and leapt without a sound
Into the waiting night. And with one bound,
With one great flexing of his wide spread wings
He broke the silence, filled each sheltered nook
With whispers, shattered stillness in a thousand
Trees, whipped up the waters at the river's edge,
Disturbed the nesting birds, called forth the owl
To hoot and hunt, the wayward alley cat
To yowl and tapped along the window panes
With leafless twigs in every passing street
Like child that runs a stick along a fence.

And sleepers stirred and turned within their beds
And house-dogs raised their heads to smell the scents
In momentary alarm. And clouds high up
Began to swing in soundless speed
Across the star specked sphere of indigo.

~ Christine Roe

Healing

8

The Stranger's Feet

Under grey skies, in chilly, evening air
I walked along, all deep in troubled thought;
my heart closed up, aching and filled with care;
my mind in rehash and rehearsal caught.

With downcast eyes, I watched my booted tread,
step after heavy step. Then suddenly
there was a glimpse of something else instead;
a shadow, someone walking next to me.

Another pair of feet beside my own,
larger than mine, in rough, brown sandals dressed.
But then they vanished, and I was alone.
Still quite alone – but somehow strangely blessed.

Why do I now look up and start to sing?
Why is my step so light? Who could it be
whose simple footsteps altered everything
in the brief moment that He walked with me?

~ Marian Van Eyk McCain

Things that Are Hidden

No one sees
the green shoot
of a tulip
emerge from the bulb
under the earth
drawn by the sunlight,
silently pierce
the surface.

No one sees
the green cells
of a Rowan tree's leaves
arrange themselves
in the hard black bud,
to burst one sunny day
into the cool spring air.

No one sees
inside the chrysalis
where the caterpillar is hidden.
How is it possible
for the pale green
undulating creature
to emerge, a while later
as a butterfly?

HEALING

No one sees
the healing under the skin
where the knife has cut.
Where the tissues
are knitting
weaving and binding
until all that is left
is a scar.

No one sees
how the darkness of grief
gradually lifts over time,
with the prompt
of a shoulder to cry on,
a listening ear,
a hand held,
and spring time.

~ Sarah Jane Toleman

Cartoon

Home from hospital with a new hip –
with Arnica Montana on my bruises and swellings –
I sleep fitfully…

It is noon in the village: I recognise the place
by its various gables and chimneys,
by the pinks of its paving stones.

The hurdy-gurdy resounds before I observe it:
gliding into view is a childhood float
complete with its cartoon cast.

A plastic rabbit with an oval face
and a pompous voice
climbs high above the rest.

I feel so uneasy about this buck
that I cannot speak. Half awake by now,
I register the pain in my bones:

how it throbs in time to the music.
At regular intervals, the buck's head sinks
into the huge, blueing dewlap –

HEALING

only to emerge with a sickening judder...
I try to wake fully but am led towards a dwarf cottage
where the cartoon menagerie waits for its feast.

I listen to the woman with the ebony hair
that sticks out from her temples.
She resembles one of those monochrome gables –

is entirely unaware that I will occupy her psyche...
The music stops: the rabbit responds with a fattened yawn.
My pain gone, I anticipate nothing but food.

A straw man limps past.
I glance out of the lattice window
in time to see the raven poised on a gatepost.

A clock strikes. I am brought back to the otherlife,
knowing that my keywords – little, and slow –
are ones that I like.

~ Jenny Johnson

Samhain Full Moon

Healing is happening; in the full moon
pulling out from behind
the black clouds, in the cold wind
blowing my hair from my eyes, the red leaves
from the Acer, in the sea, blessing
the rocky shore. Life
moves through her brilliant cycles, and this now
is the beginning of the dark time. We stand and hold hands
in a loving circle. We mark this moment.
We are turning inwards,
settling down, connecting, moving
into the earth, for healing
and for transformation. We will wait for
the light of inner knowing and becoming.
Like the tiny seeds turning in the dark soil
awaiting the warmth of Spring,
we know we shall grow.
We will become stronger, clearer, truer
and all the while, the moon will cycle onwards
endlessly, in the black sky, while the wind blows
and the sea blesses the shore.

~ Bryony Rogers

HEALING

Blessing
(South Island, New Zealand)

A whole flock of birds is flying
inside me. I am bending down
to a clear blue lake
and splashing water over myself. This moment

stopped in time. I speak a blessing
for myself and for this being of blue
water. The mountains watch me, stepping off
into a sky where small white clouds

drift. It is coming on evening. I sit
on a wooden log, and breathe deeply
on fresh clean air. Up above
a hawk circles. Dark brown

wings outstretched, the body so
full of precision and knowing. I feel
my body

dissolving into the blue field
of the lake, the healing
water. I am

made new.

~ Bryony Rogers

Each Sparkling Star –

is an incandescent snowflake
Or a
drop of milk
5000,000,000 years of
    lactating herds
Auroch bison
Wooly mammoth
Saber toothed cats
Jittery impala
Fireflies and phosphorous
You and I
    Momentary
Looking out and down
Talking
    Imagining
Singing
We huddle together and tell of
how it all began
over and over.

HEALING

At length myriad breasted
Goddess turns many armed
    Bodhisattva
That looking down heard
Wearisome cries
    and in prolonged compassion
wept a deep pool
At the heart of which
    a gestation of light
shivered and a seed-leaf sprang forth
a hand strove skyward
    a foot pushed down firmly
Love ascended
    Her many petalled flower
Throne
    And each star rang clear
    a splendour of tiny bells.

Alongside what is irksome
thrawnly wrought
innately pain filled
    is that which helps heal
hallows
    lights a signal beacon home

~ Richard Meyers

A Piece of Sky

From where I lie
I see a piece of sky
between the houses.
In the evening
it is striped grey and lemon.
Distant trees are silhouettes.
Birds sing their last duets.
The night is dark and long.

The morning sky is blue,
pale above the trees.
Later purple clouds bruise
and darken the room.
Wind lashes rain on the window pane.

The sun appears, the room lights up,
rainbows dance on the walls.
The sky is bleached by the brightness
and I am warmed and healed.

~ Sarah Jane Toleman

Humanity's Environmental Cruelty and Destruction

9

Moon Landing

It is deep dark; the day has fled,
and all the world has gone to bed.
Save for night creatures on the prowl:
the rasping fox, the ghostly owl.

The skies step back to let you shine.
And, as your silver gaze meets mine,
my arms outstretched, I call your name,
To ask forgiveness for my shame.

Shame of my kind, who lost the plot
when we, in clumsy haste, forgot
humility and reverence,
our age-old, pagan deference

to the Earth Goddess, and to you,
my sister Moon. What can I do?
except to make apology
for foolish, brute humanity.

Yes, I, too, cheered in pride that day
we stole your virgin soul away.
This is my vain and boastful race.
That was my boot upon your face.

No answer comes. Impassive, proud,
you sweep from view, behind a cloud.

~ Marian Van Eyk McCain

Thoughts on Leaving the Yorkshire Dales

O you ancient rolling hills
What are your thoughts as you recline serenely around us?
Can you feel the climate changing,
the pollution we have caused as you breathe the air and bathe
 in the rain?
We owe our survival to you:
We have nestled at your feet for thousands of years.
You have sheltered, clothed and fed us
and now we pollute your springs and rivers,
steal peat from your moors,
blast rocks from your faces and
take trees from your forests until none remain.
You have watched us farm your lower slopes,
build houses and factories in your valleys,
carve roads and railways through your dales, only
to leave them abandoned as we build 'bigger and better' elsewhere.
Are your bones stirring with fear?
Do you wake up choking with the fumes of fossil fuels?
Are we the bane of your lives?
Have we bled you to death?
Or do you regard this as another phase in your evolution,
knowing that it will pass, that nature will find a balance and
 reassert itself,
when man is no longer a threat to the earth.

~ Joan Angus

Potatoes and Plastic

I have been digging potatoes,
What fun!
They lurk in the soil
Like naughty children hiding.
When I find one I swear
It has a broad grin on its face.
'Gotcha' I say, grinning too.
Potatoes and earth conspiring together
To produce such magic.

And then – I find the other –
It s different.
Oh, it is not death that is the enemy,
Death, which gently takes and recycles,
It is this.
Unlike you, me, houses, mountains,
Bluebells and books,
Created from earth, returnable to earth,
This modern obscenity is both unliving and undying.
It needs no 'sell-by-date'
'Will-not-rot' is its trademark
This paltry synthetic by-product
Of human irresponsible ingenuity
Leers at me from the soil.
Our human nemesis.

~ Grace Blindell

Rhetorical Questions

There's no new way
to place a robin on a page and make
it catch the eye. And that is that. Robins have sat
on every single twig in Christendom, by now,
so who am I to try
a new arrangement? Why not just buy
a box of cards from Woolworth's like the other eighty-five percent?
Why can't I be content
to sit, like Auntie Joan at her old oak
table, love and goodwill unbounded –
despite her aching, osteo-arthritic hips –
totally surrounded
by rolling seas of giftwrap and fake holly,
trying to tie gold bows with those dear, palsied fingertips,
writing names, in spidery hand, on tiny tags
with robins (on their usual twigs) and jolly,
fat santas with bulging bags, reindeer in snow, mistletoe
– all of that? With ne-er a thought of landfill, ozone holes,
     felled trees, she's here,
at her post, enjoying this season for the ninetieth year.

HUMANITY'S ENVIRONMENTAL CRUELTY AND DESTRUCTION

Why can't I revel, like my neighbours, in
the bright, electric, made-in-China, red-white-green graffiti scrawl
and jerky-footed santas going nowhere on the wall?
What good is it to celebrate
the coming of a saviour whose word
no-one ever really heard,
and in whose name, in these few minutes I sit here
trying to place a robin redbreast on a page,
another dozen breasts, a thousand miles away
are bloodstained red by war. What more
insane and horrible than that?
How can I put it all
together in a picture not already done
by some sweet poet less tongue-tied than I?
No. Let it lie. Soon all the pain
will drain away, down the year's last, frozen slope.
And I can rise to meet
a new year full of hope. Meanwhile, put on the silly hat,
the silly smile, and do the best I can.
Outside my window, in the grey December dawn
a robin sings
the same familiar song, forever new, forever sweet.

~ Marian Van Eyk McCain

Binsey Poplars

Felled 1879

My aspens dear, whose airy cages quelled,
Quelled or quenched in leaves the leaping sun,
All felled, felled, are all felled;
    Of a fresh and following folded rank
        Not spared, not one
        That dandled a sandalled
        Shadow that swam or sank
On meadow ans river and wind-wandering weed-winding bank.

O if we but knew what we do
        When we delve or hew –
    Hack and rack the growing green!
        Since country is so tender
    To touch, her being so slender,
    That, like this sleek and seeing ball
    But a prick will make no eye at all,
        Where we, even where we mean
        To mend her we end her.
        When we hew or delve:
After-comers cannot guess the beauty been.
    Ten or twelve, only ten or twelve
        Strokes of havoc unselve
        The sweet especial scene,
        Rural scene, a rural scene,
        Sweet especial rural scene.

~ Gerard Manley Hopkins

HUMANITY'S ENVIRONMENTAL CRUELTY AND DESTRUCTION

The Boss's Revenge
The Dangers of Genetic Engineering

God moved in a mysterious way
His wonders to perform.
But then Monsanto seized the day.
GM became the norm

"We've cracked the mystery!" they said,
"And now WE'LL make the rules,
"We'll engineer their daily bread."
Oh dear, the silly fools.

For what those fellows hadn't gauged
About the King of Kings
Was how He hates to be upstaged
In terms of making things.

Now all of us will get the blame,
Not just the scientists,
And every human being's name
May well be on the list.

We'll know not method, time nor day
Of that fierce, cleansing storm.
He moves in a mysterious way
His wonders to perform.

~ Marian Van Eyk McCain

Grandma's Story

In my day there were four –
December to February, bare trees,
the world dormant; silent
except for the sky transport
trailing evil gas clouds
and the noise of road machines
puffing out poison.
It became so cold that
water turned to ice, snow fell,
we wore coats and gloves.

Then Spring; and slowly
the world awoke to
dawn chorus of birds,
frogspawn in the pond,
rainbows and pale sunshine,
everything green and yellow.

June to August, you could rely
on all of it growing and ripening.
Most years it was warm,
– but not stifling like this.
Imagine – if it wasn't warm enough
we travelled abroad.

September – harvesting
the crops we planted in the spring.
Leaves changing from green
to golds and browns.
Animals bedding down
in warm nests for the winter.

Yes, four. Seasons they were called.
Then – you wouldn't remember –
the time of change;
imperceptibly at first –
succeeding hot dry summers,
but then the catalytic storms began,
the old rhythm gone for ever.

Of course, sitting here,
looking out at this barren landscape,
waiting for the monsoon,
it's hard for you to imagine.

~ Heather Shute

Power 1

Human creature, do you think you have power?
Can you melt rock,
draw it up, red and molten,
shoot it out in cascading yellow and orange,
a river of heat,
burning all in its path?
Can you push up mountain ranges
and grind them down?

You break the rock.
You build the tower.
The barriers you build
demonstrate your power.
But over time the walls break up.
Small people take the stone
to build homes.

The wind and rain beat down,
eat the mortar, loosen stone.
The seeds find niches
in which to grow
and burst the stones apart.

HUMANITY'S ENVIRONMENTAL CRUELTY AND DESTRUCTION

You cut down trees
and reshape hills.
You modify even the source of life
but can you stop the seed from growing rampant
when your back is turned?

You tame the wolf,
kill off insects with your poison,
gorge yourself on fish
'til you empty the ocean.
But can you stop the dog biting?
the poison you make poisoning your children?
Feed yourself when the soil is barren?

The oceans will replenish,
the insects evolve
and the wolves regain freedom.

You reign is but for an instant.
Life rules infinitely.

~ Sarah Jane Toleman

Conclusion

CONCLUSION

Creative Spirit

I am in the air we breathe.
I am in the sun, which lights our day,
dappled through leaves of trees.
I am in the moon, moving the tides,
the stars traversing the night sky.

I am in the earth, feeding the seed,
that grows, flowers, wilts
and dies, to become earth.
I am the pollen on the bees' knees,
fertilising the flowers to make those seeds
to become plants which feed us; and trees,
that give us the air we breathe.

I am in the birdsong,
the tigers' stripes, the fishes' gills,
and dewdrops on the spider's web.
I am the flowing of the river, the colours
of the rainbow, the soul of the rock.

I am the diversity of life forms,
life cycles of living things,
the balance of nature.

I am the laughter in your eyes. I am
in your joys, sorrows, hopes and fears.
I am in your health and sickness.
I am in your anger and you are in mine.
You are in my peace and I am in yours.
When you love me, then you love yourself.

We are in the music we make, the words we say.
We are in our dreams and schemes;
the houses we build, the children we birth.
When we abuse these treasures,
we abuse ourselves.
When we kill, we kill ourselves.

We are the Universe, changing and renewing,
constantly flowing, enfolding, enriching, sustaining.

~ Joan Angus

Biographies

BIOGRAPHIES

Joan Angus grew up in the Yorkshire countryside, roaming the hills when she wasn't at school. From an early age she felt she belonged to Nature's community.

She went to college in Liverpool where she trained to become an Occupational Therapist and moved south following her husband's job opportunities. They raised their two children in Hampshire, where she now lives with her second husband and their collie dog, at the edge of the South Downs.

After retirement she became interested in genealogy and has self-published three novels based on the family history of her paternal grandmother.

She has been a member of GreenSpirit for around twenty years, much of that serving on the Council.

Cornish poet and author Roselle Angwin has been leading the holistic 'Fire in the Head' creative and reflective writing programme for 29 years. As an eco-writer and transpersonal counsellor, she also leads 'The Wild Ways' outdoor workshops and retreats designed to help deepen our sense of intimacy with the other-than-human and the sacred. Courses take place in beautiful wildish locations in Britain and France, and online.

Roselle's publications include poetry, fiction and narrative non-fiction. Her new book *A Spell in the Forest – tongues in trees* is due out in June 2021. She has been described as 'a poet of the bright moment... whose own sources of creative inspiration are her native Westcountry, the Scottish islands, a Brittany forest, and a highly individual blend of Celtic myth and metaphysics, psychology, native British shamanic and Zen thinking'.

www.fire-in-the-head.co.uk
www.thewildways.co.uk
www.57billion.org
roselle-angwin.blogspot.com

Ruth Barton's poems reflect her deep regard for the natural world. Most mornings she greets the day marvelling at the beauty and complexity of what she calls the work of the Great Creator. It's what moves her to write most of her poems. Her almost finished novel is different. Her imagination runs wild as her characters experience the unexpected.

In 1982, Ruth and her family moved into a wooden bungalow on an acre of land. They developed the plot into a plant nursery. When the children left home there was more time for writing about the antics of their Pot-bellied pig, chickens, ducks and goats. Ruth's holidays in Scotland inspired her to write about mountains, lochs and weather.

Ruth claims the accolade of being a descendant of Robert Cawdrey who compiled the first English dictionary in 1604.

Grace Blindell was born 1921. She nursed in London during the war. Subsequently nursed and taught English in France, Singapore, Malaya, Nigeria, Gaza strip and was awarded a Red Cross medal for work in Malaya.

She was in California when she first heard Matthew Fox speak about Creation Centred Spirituality, later to become GreenSpirit. She came to London and became involved at St James Piccadilly, helping in the office. She remembers Matthew Fox coming to speak there.

The Rev Dr June Boyce-Tillman MBE read music at Oxford University and is Professor Emerita of Applied Music at the University of Winchester and an Extra-ordinary Professor at North West University, South Africa. She is an Anglican priest. Her interests are in music education, theology and wellbeing through music. Her international one woman shows concentrate on spiritual themes and the lives of the mystics such as Hildegard of Bingen. She is an international hymn writer – *A Rainbow to Heaven*. She lectures internationally and is concerned with radical musical inclusion, composing large-scale works for cathedrals such as Winchester, Norwich and Southwark involving professional musicians, school and community choirs, and children and adults with disabilities and schoolchildren. She is editing a series on Music and Spirituality for Peter Lang including: *Experiencing Music-Restoring the Spiritual* and the edited collection *Queering Freedom: Music, Identity and Spirituality*. She founded Music, Spirituality and Wellbeing International (www.mswinternational.org) http://www.impulse-music.co.uk/juneboyce-tillman/

Chris Clarke (22.02.1946 – 16.04.2019): Chris's formidable intellect took him to international recognition in the fields of General Relativity and Cosmology, along with a chair in Applied Mathematics at York University, 1986 – 1999.

His lifelong passion for humanity and justice led to deep involvement with the Christian faith from his conversion as a student in the 1960s, to involvement with Scientists Against Nuclear Arms, and then the environmental movement through involvement with Creation Spirituality from its inception. He was chair of Creation Spirituality/GreenSpirit following his departure from academic life, through disillusionment with the direction universities were taking, in 1999. As well as mathematical works, he has published on philosophy and the spiritual potential of the environment movement in the following books.

Knowing, Being, and Doing: New Foundations for Consciousness Studies, 2013. Imprint Academic.

Weaving the Cosmos: science, religion and ecology, 2010. O Books.

Ways of Knowing. Science and Mysticism Today (Edited), 2005. Imprint Academic.

Living in Connection. Theory and Practice of the New World View,

2002. Creation Spirituality Books: Warmister.

Reality through the Looking Glass. Science and Awareness in the Post Modern World, 1996. Floris Books.

And the posthumously published collection of the tree focused blog he wrote during his last few years, while contending with the insidious onset of Alzheimer's.

Wisdom and Isness: Deep reflections on living in the moment, 2019.

For more see: www.scispirit.com and https://blog.scispirit.com/search/label/tributes

Miranda Cox: I started writing poetry when I went to New Zealand during a year off before uni to visit my Kiwi mother's family and learn how to be independent. I was lonely and had some painful romantic liaisons and writing helped me express my feelings.

Back in the UK I studied law at Kent university, volunteered for a homeless peoples' charity, studied and practised acupuncture then psychotherapy and moved from near Taunton to Bideford to live with and marry my husband.

I was a green councillor on Northam Town and Torridge District councils for seven and four years respectively, loving and wanting to protect nature and the environment.

Throughout these times and especially from being in writing groups locally I have written mostly poetry but also some short stories and a novel and enjoy the creativity and release of being expressive in this way.

Christine Roe Cripps (1923-2020) was born in 1923, Christine experienced many changes in our world. She had a deep faith in God. Much of her poetry reflects her faith, and her love of creation, of all things on earth. She loved her family, her six children and wider family, the many friends she made along the way, animals, birds and insects – especially frogs! She loved her garden.

BIOGRAPHIES

Throughout her long life – she died aged 96 in January 2020 – Christine continued to learn, and master new skills – including computers, the Internet, and email. In addition to poetry she wrote about growing up before the War, and of her trip to Canada in her 80s – tracing the steps of her missionary great-uncle in the Yukon! She wrote from an early age, poems for us as children, and her many diverse interests. Her acute sense of humour, love and wonder, show clearly in her poems.

Dr Vivianne Crowley is a writer, psychologist and an international teacher of mindfulness and Earth-based spiritual traditions. She is a member of the Department of Psychology, Nottingham Trent University, UK, where she specialises in the psychology of religion and spirituality, and was formerly Lecturer in Psychology of Religion at King's College, University of London. Her research interests include contemporary Paganism, women religious leaders and religious experience. She is the author of many books on contemporary Paganism and on Jungian psychology, including the best-selling *Wicca: The Old Religion in the Modern World* and *Jung: Journey of Transformation*. Her forthcoming book *You were Wild Once*, an exploration of green spirituality and magic, will be published by Century-Random House in 2021.

George Eliot (1819-1880): Was known by this pen name. She was born as Mary Ann(e) / Marian Evans and was a leading writer of her time. She lived with her partner George Henry Lewes between 1854 and 1878 and later married John Cross in 1880.

Gerard Manley Hopkins, SJ (1844-1889): Born in Stratford, Essex, Hopkins became a Jesuit priest. He wrote some influential poetry which was not published until 1918, after his death. He died in Dublin.

Jenny Johnson was born in 1945 in Bristol, where she attended The Red Maids' School (now Redmaids High School). She has written poetry all her life and has also created eighty community dances. With her husband Noel Harrower, she ran GreenSpirit groups during the 1990s and in the early years of the twenty-first century, first in Nottingham and later in Exeter. For several years, she worked as a Reiki therapist at The Quiet Mind Centre in Exmouth, which provided free treatment for people on low incomes. A sample of Jenny's poetry can be found on her website – www.jennyjohnsondancerpoet.net – as can a full list of her dances and musical sources. Her latest poetry collection, *Selected Poems: Revised & New*, was published by Brimstone Press in 2013. During the past four years, she has written a sequence of forty-two poems based on dreams: *Dreamlines* seeks a publisher!

Jenny Joyce and Alan Whear have been singing together and with friends since the folk revival of the 60s and 70s. When they joined a group of meditators exploring earth-based spirituality, they were inspired to create hymns and songs celebrating the living earth and our connection with all life.

They were early members of the GreenSpirit local group in Ascot, and took part in events celebrating the festivals of the Celtic year, bringing music and song to welcome the turning of the year.

The grace included here was written to celebrate Lammas, festival of the first fruits. It is sung to *La Morisque*, a renaissance dance tune brought up to date by the Albion Band.

David Kelf grew up in Gorleston near the rolling sea: I spent a lot of time near the sea and outdoors, including many a ramble across open fields listening to the skylarks above, while my mother played tennis. Angling was one of my early interests.

When I left school in 1965 I joined the Met Office and in

1973 I moved to the Hydrographic Office in Taunton. I was able to follow many avenues of interest including my main ones of cross-country running, weather observing, labyrinth making and I became a voluntary emissary for the Schumacher College where I met Satish Kumar.

Since retiring I have been involved with Dowsing and have moved back to Gorleston. I have led walks along the Michael and Mary living currents from Hopton to Lands End in this country, which gets me out into our wonderful countryside and there have been many church visits along the way. I am currently the vice-chair of the Great Yarmouth InterFaith and Belief local network.

DH Lawrence (1885-1930): David Herbert Lawrence was born in Eastwood, Nottinghamshire and was educated locally, leading to his qualification as a teacher in 1906.

He was troubled with recurring serious illness most of his life, which caused him to leave his teaching post in Croydon in 1912. Soon after, he eloped with Frieda Weekley to Germany where they stayed until 1914 when war broke out.

Returning to England, they married at Kensington Registry Office. They stayed until 1925 while his illness became worse, then returned to Europe.

Lawrence was a prolific writer.

Nigel Lees was, for 30 years, a chemistry information specialist in various organisations and published a number of articles and books on his work. Although now retired he is still very passionate about science and tries very hard to write creatively on the connections he perceives between science, art and spirituality. He has written a few articles for GreenSpirit, is a keen wildlife gardener and vegetable grower.

Marian van Eyk McCain: Plato said "Every man, before he dies, should do four things: father a son, build a house, write a book, and plant a tree". He didn't mention what women should do, of course. But Marian has built a house (out of mud bricks and recycled timber), written seven books, birthed two children and planted hundreds of trees. She also published dozens of articles, plus short stories and poems, and co-edits the GreenSpirit magazine.

Originally from Devon in the south-west of England, Marian has travelled extensively and lived on four continents. She has a BSW from Melbourne University and an MA in East-West Psychology from the CIIS San Francisco and worked as a social worker and as a transpersonal psychotherapist in private practice. Returning to her roots after retirement, she now lives with her soulmate/husband in a Devon village where her current project is the co-creation of an elders eco-cohousing community.

Sister Kay (Ann Catharine) McMullen, SNDdeN (July 18, 1939 – March 12, 2018). Born in Oakland, Kay entered the Sisters of Notre Dame in 1959. She taught in Notre Dame schools and received her bachelor's degree in music from College of Notre Dame, Belmont, and later, a Montessori diploma and Master's degree in Early Childhood Education.

In the 1980s, Sr. Kay volunteered with the Monterey County AIDS Project and John XXIII HIV/AIDS Services, helping with AIDS education and peer counseling, and frequently accompanying those who were dying.

In the past four months, the courage and grace Sr. Kay showed in dealing with glioblastoma, an especially aggressive form of cancer, was an inspiration to everyone who knew her. She, who was so gifted with words, became unable to speak or communicate in any written form. She still found ways to express her care and appreciation for others until she passed away in 2008.

BIOGRAPHIES

Richard Meyers was born in 1947 in the London Borough of Islington. His last working years were based at Islington Ecology Centre and he died in an Islington hospital in October 2013, and so his life came full circle.

Most of Richard's childhood was spent in the new town of Crawley where he developed his love of the natural world through the freedom he was given to explore the surrounding countryside and Worth forest. Richard was entirely self educated, having left school at the age of 15.

Richard found huge fulfillment in his work in nature conservancy. As Outreach Officer at Islington Ecology Centre he shared his wide knowledge and delight in the natural world with a wide variety of community groups with huge generosity of spirit.

Richard became very interested in Creation Spirituality in the 1990's and during a period of unemployment he volunteered at St. James's Church, Piccadilly in the early years of GreenSpirit.

Helen Moore is an award-winning British ecopoet, socially engaged artist and outdoor educator based in SW England. She has published three poetry collections, *Hedge Fund, And Other Living Margins* (Shearsman Books, 2012); ECOZOA (Permanent Publications, 2015), acclaimed as "a milestone in the journey of ecopoetics", and in which her poem 'glory be to Gaia' is included; and *The Mother Country* (Awen Publications, 2019) exploring aspects of British colonial history. Helen offers an online mentoring programme, Wild Ways to Writing, supporting a creative writing journey into deeper Nature connection, and leads workshops in a range of locations. Helen is currently collaborating with Cape Farewell on RiverRun, a science-informed arts project examining algal blooms in Poole Harbour. She has recently received an award from the Royal Literary Fund to support her work, and has a poem nominated for this year's Forward Prize. www.helenmoorepoet.com

Ellis Mortimer: I am 11 years old and live in rural north Dorset. I have just left Primary school and will be starting secondary in September.

I have a great love of nature and outdoors, I love to write poetry and am greatly influenced by the natural world. We spend a lot of our spare time exploring the many footpaths around our beautiful village, and I collect many things I find along the way (most of which is stored in my shed!) I enjoy spending time with my friends from the surrounding villages.

I have lived in Dorset all of my life and I am very fond of my surroundings, however, my grandparents live in North Devon, by the sea and I have a great love for that area too.

When I am not outside, you can find me in my room, drawing an original character or reading my favourite books.

Ian Mowll has worked in financial markets, for homeless people and in mental health. He is now the Coordinator of GreenSpirit and an Interfaith Minister conducting ceremonies for people of all faiths and none. He also has a passion for the Universe Story (that is the story as revealed by science from the big bang through to today) and its implications for our lives.

Chris Newsam lives in Malton, North Yorkshire with his wife Janice, mother in law Edith and Saluki dog Sophie. A Quaker for some 20 years with an open and inclusive and eclectic spiritual outlook. Chris has a passion for peacemaking and social justice and has been active in many campaigns. He is actively interested in helping to protect the natural environment and has been a member of GreenSpirit for more than a decade, currently serving on the national council which administers the charity and helps to steer it in fulfilling its role of increasing knowledge and passion for all things green. Chris occasionally writes poetry and enjoys reading and walking the beautiful landscape of North Yorkshire including the rugged coastline.

Sue Proffitt lives by the coast in South Devon. Writing poetry is central to her life and is an exploration of the beauty and mystery of the more-than-human world, and of our complex human relationship with it. She has an MA in Creative Writing from the University of Bath Spa and has been published in a number of magazines and journals. Her first collection, *Open After Dark*, was published by Oversteps in 2017. Her second collection, *The Lock-Picker*, will be coming out late this year, published by Palewell Press. In 2018 she was awarded a Hawthornden Fellowship.

Gull Dawn was originally published in *Open After Dark* (Oversteps, 2017).

Bryony Rogers is a Writer, Singer, Coach and Therapeutic Film-maker, living in Lancashire. She has published many poems over the years, in *Earth Pathways* publications and various magazines. Her most recent poetry collection, *Wilderness Renewal*, exploring Spiritual Nature Connection, is available as an eBook for £6 from her at bryonytree@gmail.com.

She also recently published a longer book, sharing the Spiritual Guidance she has been receiving for the past 23 years, since her Awakening experience living at the Findhorn Community. The book, *The Golden Road: My Journey with Spirit*, has beautiful prose, channelled from Source, interwoven with full colour Nature photographs from Scotland, England and New Zealand. *The Golden Road: My Journey with Spirit* is available from Amazon, as both paperback and eBook.

You can see more about Bryony's work at www.songofawakening. org.uk and on Facebook – Heartsong Sacred Singing and Meditation, Wilderness Renewal, Nature as Medicine and Moving Essence pages.

Rev Dr Margie Schneider has a bachelor's degree in Multi-disciplinary Studies, Master of Arts in Religion, and a Master of Divinity from Liberty University.

Is certified in Eco-Art Therapy from Project NatureConnect. Ordained at the The School of Peace as an Interfaith Minister with a focus in Ecospirituality.

Is ordained as an Animal Chaplain and Pet Bereavement Facilitator, as well as has received a Doctorate in Humane Religious Studies from Emerson Institute.

Presently working towards receiving a Creation Spirituality Certification from Global Ministries University; and For fourteen years, ran a non-profit animal sanctuary, while raising five adopted developmentally delayed children, which, eventually led to the establishing of a non-profit, called Heart-To-Heart All Creatures Ministry, which is both online and local.

Heather Shute enjoyed writing essays at school, and as an adult wrote mainly various magazine articles and some short stories, and (to her shame, and for the money!) even contributed the 'speech bubbles' for illustrated stories in girls' comics.

She began to write poems in the 1980s, after joining a creative writing group at Braziers Park community in Oxfordshire. She writes in fits and starts, when she feels she has something to say, has published one or two poems in anthologies, and has a go at poetry competitions.

She lives in a Cotswold village with three small dogs who help with her volunteer fundraising for the charity Medical Detection Dogs – which is her raison d'etre.

She also enjoys working in the local library as a volunteer, and with the Berks Bucks & Oxon Wildlife trust. She has a special interest in Water Vole conservation, and monitoring the Swifts when those magical birds return to breed in Britain.

BIOGRAPHIES

Rabindranath Tagore (1861-1941): Born in Kolkata, India, He was an artist, poet, writer and musician who had a great reforming influence on Bengali art, music and literature. He died in Jorasanko Thakurban, Kolkata.

Sarah-Jane Toleman: I have lived in the North East of Scotland for 30 years, though I was brought up in the tree lands of Hampshire. I have always been drawn to green things from toddling by my Granny and Mum along the hedgerows to taking long country walks in the highlands of Deeside. From these experiences come the inspiration for my writing. As well as writing I love to draw and from time to time I illustrate my poems.

I have two grown up daughters and a black cat and I work as a teacher of English as An Additional Language. As well as walking in the countryside I like to grow things in my garden and read.

Peter Watkins is a Suffolk poet living on the Stour Estuary. Many of his poetic motifs arise from the gentle landscape and the slow rivers of Suffolk in which he finds divinity, solace and inspiration. He is interested in the 'redress of poetry'; that is the capacity of poems to push back against the vicissitudes of life. His first collection Enough to Love a Multitude is published by Eye Wild Books. Peter is co-founder of the arts and mental health charity Inside Out Community.

GreenSpirit Resources

GreenSpirit Book Series & Other Resources

We hope you have enjoyed reading this book, and that it has whetted your appetite to read more in this series and discover the many and varied ways in which green spirituality can be expressed in every single aspect of our lives and culture.

You may also wish to visit our website, which has a members area, information about GreenSpirit's annual events, book reviews and much more: **www.greenspirit.org.uk**

GreenSpirit
magazine

GreenSpirit magazine is free for members and is published in both print and electronic form. Each issue includes essential topics connected with Earth-based spirituality. It honours Nature as a great teacher, celebrates the creativity and interrelatedness of all life and of the cosmos, affirms biodiversity and human differences, and honours the prophetic voice of artists.

Find out more at www.greenspirit.org.uk

"For many of us, it's the spirit running through that limitless span of green organisations and ideas that anchors all the work we do. And 'GreenSpirit' is an invaluable source of insight, information and inspiration."
— Jonathon Porritt.

Other titles in the GreenSpirit Book Series

What is Green Spirituality? Edited by Marian Van Eyk McCain

All Our Relations: GreenSpirit Connections with the More-than-Human World. Edited by Marian Van Eyk McCain

The Universe Story in Science and Myth. By Greg Morter and Niamh Brennan

Rivers of Green Wisdom: Exploring Christian and Yogic Earth Centred Spirituality. By Santoshan (Stephen Wollaston)

Pathways of Green Wisdom: Discovering Earth Centred Teachings in Spiritual and Religious Traditions. Edited by Santoshan (Stephen Wollaston)

Deep Green Living. Edited by Marian Van Eyk McCain

The Rising Water Project: Real Stories of Flooding, Real Stories of Downshifting. Compiled by Ian Mowll

Dark Nights of the Green Soul: From Darkness to New Horizons. Edited by Ian Mowll and Santoshan (Stephen Wollaston)

Awakening to Earth-Centred Consciousness: Selection from GreenSpirit magazine Edited by Ian Mowll and Santoshan (Stephen Wollaston)

GreenSpirit Reflections Compiled by Santoshan (Stephen Wollaston)

More details on GreenSpirit's website

Free for members ebook editions

GreenSpirit
Path to a New Consciousness
Edited by Marian Van Eyk McCain

Only by bringing our thinking back into balance with feeling, intuition and awareness and by grounding ourselves in a sense of the sacred in all things can we achieve a new level of consciousness.

Green spirituality is the key to a new, twenty-first century consciousness. And here is the most comprehensive book ever written on green spirituality.

Published by Earth Books
ISBN 978-1-84694-290-7
282 pages

Meditations with Thomas Berry
With additional material by Brian Swimme
Selected by June Raymond

Selected and arranged by June Raymond, especially for GreenSpirit Books, this is a collection of profound and inspiring quotations from one of the most important voices of our times, the late Thomas Berry, author, geologian, cultural historian and lover of the Earth.

Published by GreenSpirit
ISBN 978-0-9552157-4-2
111 pages

Printed in Great Britain
by Amazon